Pale Bird, Spouting Fire

Akron Series in Poetry

Akron Series in Poetry
Elton Glaser, Editor

Barry Seiler, *The Waters of Forgetting*

Raeburn Miller, *The Comma After Love: Selected Poems of Raeburn Miller*

William Greenway, *How the Dead Bury the Dead*

Jon Davis, *Scrimmage of Appetite*

Anita Feng, *Internal Strategies*

Susan Yuzna, *Her Slender Dress*

Raeburn Miller, *The Collected Poems of Raeburn Miller*

Clare Rossini, *Winter Morning with Crow*

Barry Seiler, *Black Leaf*

William Greenway, *Simmer Dim*

Jeanne E. Clark, *Ohio Blue Tips*

Beckian Fritz Goldberg, *Never Be the Horse*

Marlys West, *Notes for a Late-Blooming Martyr*

Dennis Hinrichsen, *Detail from* The Garden of Earthly Delights

Susan Yuzna, *Pale Bird, Spouting Fire*

Susan Yuzna

Pale Bird, Spouting Fire

The University of Akron Press
Akron, Ohio

for my mother, Ruthe Grandokken Paczkowski

Not 'Revelation'—'tis—that waits,
But our unfurnished eyes—

—Emily Dickinson

Acknowledgments:
Alaska Quarterly Review: "The Cage."
Blue Skunk Companion: "The Way the Body."
HEAT 10: "Poem for the Black Whore in That Bar on Pike Street" and "The Telephonist."
The Laurel Review: "The Confession."
North Dakota Quarterly: "With Ferns around Her Face" and "Women at Fifty."

My gratitude to the MacDowell, U Cross, and Yaddo colonies for residencies that made these poems possible. I would also like to thank Robert W. Lewis, Chair, and the Executive Committee of the English Department at the University of North Dakota for release time to work on these poems.

All inquiries and permission requests should be addressed to the Publisher, The University of Akron Press, 374B Bierce Library, Akron, Ohio 44325-1703.

Library of Congress Cataloging-in-Publication-Data
Yuzna, Susan, 1949–
Pale bird, spouting fire / Susan Yuzna.—1st ed.
p. cm. — (Akron series in poetry)
ISBN 1-884836-62-3 — ISBN 1-884836-63-1 (pa)
I. Title. II. Series.
811'.54—dc21
00-041153

Manufactured in the United States of America
The paper used in this publication meets the minimum requirements of American National Standard for Information Sciences—Permanence of Paper for Printed Library Materials, ANSI Z39.48-1984.∞
First Edition

Contents

One

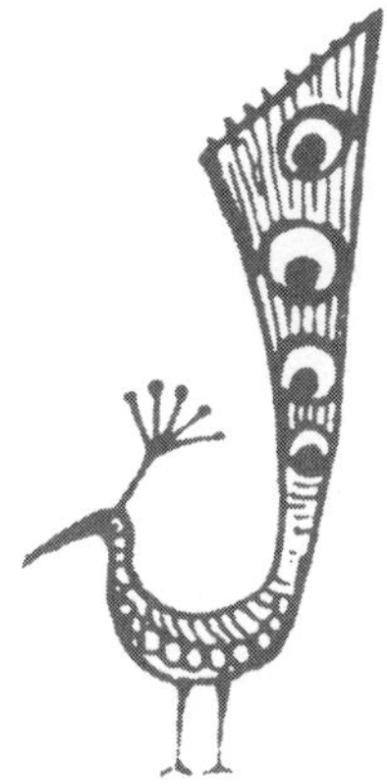

The Cage

My father was named for St. Francis of Assisi,
a man so pure he could speak with the animals.

But my father heard only the noise people make.

I have come back
to the arms that held me in the old days.

To the Big Horn Mountains, where there are
sheep at my window, deer on the path.

And a moon so full, the mountains seem to
lap against the sky—a moon so full—

ooh, ooh, ooh, what a little moonlight can do
to you—

A moon so full, the cage is visible.

Quietly, the animal spirits laugh.

My father is also here, cradled by the moon.

Can he see me now? Can he hear me at last?

The animal spirits announce an arabesque.

So it is written.

In the lexicon of coyote, eagle, bear, egret, bison,
it is written. *Ye who have ears, let him hear.*

Tomorrow, my son will be born.

In September, under a full moon,
he will put on his elegant skin.

His name, the skull of an animal, pulled down over his face.

Golden Gate

Who cares about words? We want explosions,
big ones, filling up the screen, blotting out,
for a thrilling moment, our lives, our deep
disappointment. We want the heaviest
of sweet drugs. Who needs the leisure of words?

Clematis. Clitoris. Eucalyptus.
Magnolia. I, too, should have praised more.
I should have lingered at the gate, feigned
exhaustion, before being tossed out, before
the drive of the flaming sword. I should have turned

to the magnolia tree, to the pink flesh
of its tiny fist, to the clitoris,
to the salted sky, to the fine, green pain
of the entire garden, and to its
frosted ghost, I should have saluted once.

Ordinary Sorrow

As far as you've come
can't be undone.
—Wislawa Szymborska

Are they big white hamsters, there, in the trees?
Albino rabbits? Or could it be snow?

The light is dim
in the office I share with Elizabeth, who prefers it so.

We do not turn on the light, and that gives
the large evergreen outside the window

a chance to grow spectral
in the dying of this, another slow January afternoon,

and I have come to love
its luminous company

all through my first, long, hard Dakota winter.
It is the sister, I'm sure, of that other tree—

the same heavy, low branches
weighted with glory, the same flow

of euphoria through my veins
as I consider the sculpted, white wings

of snow—maternal
in their fullness, as once

I was, waiting for the one, deep inside, who would come
to mean more than anything, more than life

itself. This is a mother speaking.
It seems I have always

been waiting, as if my life were yet to begin, and now
that it's nearly done, I remain

much the same—except for a few, one or two
stupendous runs.

Of the stallions, I name no names. I give
only the character of the initial.

A hook. Half
of a circle, broken by a line.

New Year's

Rather than winter, let us consider
Jerome: was he a saint, a cowboy with
spurs, or a freckle-faced young hooligan?

The story is open-ended, it's up
for grabs. The scene can shift to lavender
shadows, to sequined lids, or to firm

thighs of snow. Outside the window, the scene
turns dull gold. Is he translating, good boy,
or is he inscribing his oversized

valentine to me? Is there a lion
sleeping at his feet? Did he inherit
the farm, then go broke, like the rest of them?

Does he dream, yet, of the desert, its grit,
that heat between the wide dazzle of sand?
Or does he dream of California, its

young, indistinguishable women, all
in a row, bent over, a crude letter
painted on each very rounded buttock?

Will the light shine through him one grievous day,
as if he were made of stained glass, as if
he were set into a window, just so?

With Ferns around Her Face

In my new place, pulling weeds, I found a fern
like your mother, the bright green heart

shaded by a far-flung bush (its berries, fat, red beads)
she would know the name of.

But you tell me she's died. Her little tree
off the balcony in Berkeley, its small, hard oranges

we could never eat. Her wisteria, her magnolia, her
transplanting the South to California

with those gnarled, arthritic hands. Madrone,
its red bark peeling off, stripping itself

for a reason (yes, always, a reason).
She could name them all

as we drove up the coast
each awkward holiday. And after, the regret

stuck in your throat, how you liked her better
when she smelled of smoke

and taught botany, back before *he*
spread his great weight over her, when she'd

come to your room and kiss you good night. *Honey,*
I'm going out. A Georgia softness to it.

Shall I describe her to you?
Leonardo's *Ginevra,* one of his many

exquisite portraits—the bright heart of a face
circled by juniper . . . *There are passages, such as*

the modeling of the eyelids, which Leonardo
never surpassed in delicacy . . .

Passages, such as your mother's
kindness, her way of treating me as your wife

when, in fact, I wasn't, when you had one
elsewhere. Her wildest of leaps

over the Baptist roots,
those hard, black seeds

peppering the soul. But look—here she is now,
come back to the very heart of it, her hands,

like those of the *Ginevra* portrait, cut off
by persons unknown. Shall I

describe her to you? The hands, such
painful claws, dropped off, camouflaged

in this scattering of pruned twigs
all around me. Her leafy face,

like an infant, no, like *my* infant, asleep
in the smooth, green heart of the world.

I lift my hands—*you see?*—they are
the missing ones, those of the silverpoint drawing,

Study of Hands, and I arrange
the ferns around her face—*like that, just so*—

then I cross the hands
over her bosom, its exploding, green

streamers, and I hold them there. I don't
even breathe. I just hold them.

The Spirit of William Speaking to the Spirit of His Wife

> *The wild deer wandring here & there*
> *Keeps the Human Soul from Care.*
> *—William Blake*

What I like about this town, Catherine,
are the deer which appear
so suddenly out of nowhere, like a vision:

strolling down the alley of Beverly,
supper time, or trotting fast
past Hilda as I open the door to call my dog—*Lola,*

loyal as you were to me, Catherine,
rising to sit at my side, those long nights
of frenzy, as I entered the vortex,

disturbed by my wild
illuminations. Now I am finally
calmed down, dear, and here I linger,

at the door of this poor creature, hoping
to prolong the tableau, for *her*
sake—there, do you hear?

The sound of sweet hooves—do not
pity me—there, beyond the tamaracks—
departing departing departing.

The Occasional Mystic

My voices have not deceived me.
—Joan of Arc

I never wanted to be
a load-bearing structure. I wanted the light
to shine straight through me.
But the call came, the king had dire need of me, and I fell
for it. I fell hard for the flattery.
Now they tell me
it's merely a neurological quirk—a series
of minor seizures in the temporal lobe.

And Hildegard, they wrote her off
as migraine. But I believe
in their vast limitation. I believe in a cosmic gear,
in choirs of angels flipping the levers. I cannot bear
the slow, whiny grind of neurosis, the fog
of the toxic. And you, O doctor of my soul, can you imagine
how real it was, how hyperreal, when, one ordinary
summer afternoon, an arrow of light
pierced the form, and that veil fell, finally, away?

I have not been so happy since.

Women at Fifty

I watch them walking around in circles.
No, not walking, but hurrying. Always
in a hurry, from long force of habit.
But no soft-faced children cling to their skirts
or pants, now. These days, it is death they flee.

As the fierce snow beats against the windows,
as the spindly trees stir in the cold, then
crack, as the steam from the pool fogs the glass
like breath, they keep walking, moving, pushing
the milk-drained breasts, the hips like shelves, forward.

Easy to slip into the third person,
the metaphor. But this is literal.

I'm at the gym, rowing my pseudoboat,
trying to push past the anger, to glide.
There was a long-coated figure outside,
this morning, on the road, leading a horse
blanketed against the snow and the cold.

I think it must be more like that: we merge,
most of us, with the ones we love. We step
lightly into landscape: horse, figure, sky,
all white, a morning in January.
We don't rage. We turn ever so quiet.

On Crazy Woman Creek

If your man is at the border, and peacocks
lose their color, what then, dark sister, what

else? If you sit on the bank, watch the white
mist rise, and long for what is gone, you will

be enveloped, completely, by white fog,
by the absence of those tiny blue eggs

you dropped into the Iowa River
so long ago. Your hands are empty now,

so give them to me, drop them here, and we
will dance out over the water, and we

will be murmuring also, as vaguely
as the water, rushing along, must speak

to the ruined moon. See? I will begin—
here, in front of you, I slip my silken

garments off, I drop my pants, and I ask
you only for mercy. See? My right breast

owns a half moon and my navel is scarred
by a tiny line crossing it—a bridge

going nowhere, the eggs stopped in their wild
descent. And look—there are a few silver

hairs in my darkest of trees, but the smoke
is rising from my fingers now, so warm

against the cold night, the stern, cratered moon—
when they burst into flame, do not draw back.

And if heads are rolling on the frontier,
if they are busy hacking each other

to pieces, it's not our concern. I am
showing you, under the nasty moon, how

I work. If I glimmer, do not step back.
If I begin to waver a little,

my outline gone slack, please, do not be so
afraid. The mansion you see before you

is not only haunted, it is also
enlarged, engorged. What I am showing you

is the briefest of clearings, is this place
between the white fog and her pasty-faced

sister, the moon. What I am trying for
is a moment—just one—of trembling grace.

Two

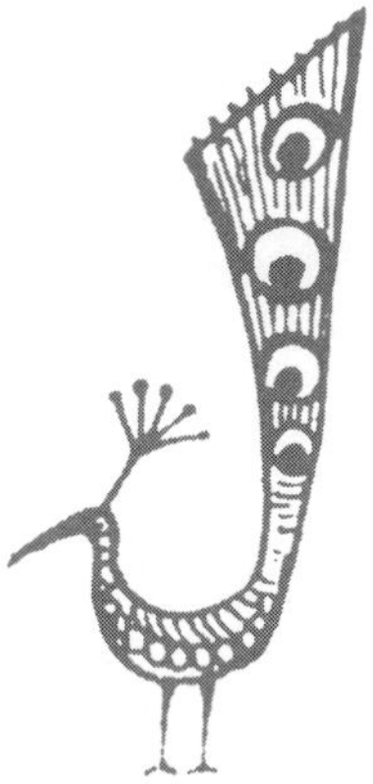

Autumn in Ohio, Thinking of James and Another

for Elton Glaser

I have flown
to this small Ohio town
to offer my poems to strangers,
to release them
as if they were pale birds
spouting fire, tiny dragon-birds, as if they would rise
into the tall October sky
at the very same moment
a golden shower of leaves
hits the pavement, and sticks. The extraordinary
coincidence of love
is like this.

It is raining
in beautiful Ohio,
and I watch the trains
from the eighth floor of the Quaker Hilton,
from the balcony of a round room
they have emptied of oats
specifically for me, I like to think, for I am
feeling silly this morning. I don't want to
put my birds in order,
nor my ducks, for that matter.
So I watch the trains,
and smoke, and think of James. I am sorry

you had such a hard time
in Minnesota, James. If it makes you
feel any better, I will confess
they have iced me over
also. I could shrink
their nasty, little heads. I could hang
the wrinkled things outside, from the rafters,
for the crows to decipher. I could put on
the black clothes and cast spells—

but the trains, down below, they keep rolling,
they keep wheezing and grunting, so why
bother? I would turn
their wet little rumps around. I would
reverse the meanness,
make them go west, again.
I would turn them romantic.

And as each car passed, I would throw
the forbidden, gilded coconuts,
and I would go on
lobbing the golden spheres
from up here, on the eighth floor—

Hey! Have another, and another,
and yet another—as the long train
snakes west, heading
for my lover. That he might find
a door, and open it—
to be knocked over, as I was, by their
perpetual coming. That he might know
the piling up of them
into a wild hill

high above him. That he might cry out
in delight, his manhood
pulsing deep inside me, his rainy, gray eyes
gone blank—*Oh, sweetheart.*

I would lift you
on the thin wings of circumstance
and twirl you around—twirl you up, up, and over
the unstoppable soil
of beautiful Ohio.

The Telephonist

for David Foster

I had my order. Not of the choirs
of angels, but of the countries we called

in the stone dead heart of the night. Japan
was a young woman's voice, *a cool river*

through a thirsty land, sliding over my bone-
tired body like an icy, blue-green

wave. Australia was next—their perpetual
joking could keep me awake. I even

made history once: for eight years, a man
had been calling his brother in the bush.

He loved me, loved my voice, my flipping of
the switches in Oakland, California,

so that, at last, it worked. But usually
I was just too tired to care. My first

graveyard shift and I was much too tired
to give a shit when the businessmen yelled

about lines down in Manila again,
as if I could stop those typhoons, as if

I could make the old crones in Manila
love us, which they didn't, or be somewhat

helpful, which they weren't. *Why don't you try*
again in two weeks? I would say (the stock

response, a polite voice, then flip the switch,
cut him off, quick, before his swearing

poisons my ear). Too tired to care
about anything, not their business dealing,

not the drunken nostalgia for a whore
known during the war—he can't remember

her name, or the place where she worked, the street
it was on, but could I help him find her?

He's never forgotten . . . I grew so tired
of phones ringing for eight hours straight.

I wanted to pull my hair out, one thin
strand at a time. It was a newly

invented circle of hell, and if you
had been there, you just might understand

why that infamous *hippie girl* rose up,
out of her chair, yanked the earphones off, and climbed

onto a counter running the length of the room
beneath our long, black switchboard, then, crawling

from station to station, pulled each cord
from its black tunnel, breaking one connection

after another, like a series of
coitus interruptus all down the board,

before they stopped her, and led her away.
She must be on LSD, said a wife

from the Alameda military base. *And she wears*
no underwear, either, added another.

That was 1970, back when Oakland
Overseas was still manual, but the hatred

of a ringing phone is with me yet.
I will stand at the center of a room

and watch the damn thing ring its little head off,
and I will grin, quite stupidly, at its

helplessness. I will walk out the door, fill
my lungs with ice, head for the far-off peaks.

I will lose myself, become one small, dark stroke
in the white stillness of snow. I'm telling you

now, it was a brand new circle of hell,
but how could we know that, then? We had jobs,

the market was tight, and the union
won us cab rides home when we worked at night.

Poem for the Black Whore in That Bar on Pike Street

We both worked the night shift, drinking, after work,
at 8 A.M. Her man, large, smiling,
sat to my left, buying me drinks. *How much*
you make an hour, girl? You be a fool
to work for that. Lookit here now, will you?

She opened her wrinkled trench coat
to show me what the big man said was true: for work,
she wore a black negligee. At the look
on my face, they both threw their heads back and laughed.
I thought pimps were mean, whores pathetic.

He put his money on the bar, signaling
the bartender for another. Then they begged off,
needing some sleep, they said, but at the door, began
laughing again. I didn't mind.
I turned to the next man.

His jaw was wired shut, making it
difficult to drink. He used a straw. What he
didn't say, I didn't ask. But whatever
my problem was, it was the same as his:
I could not speak of it, my grief.

So, speechless, I walked up the hill, toward home.
A lovely light was out and about, but even that
could not cheer me. I was playing
a closed-down carnival, acting my own ghost, kicking
the rain-soaked trash, feeling unloved.

I know they thought me perverse, ungrateful.
My letter of resignation began:
One must have a mind of winter
To work at the Bon Marché,
And have been cold a long time . . .

My friends later told me, laughingly,
there was a meeting of management.
that the MBAs were confounded,
utterly, by Stevens. Of course. Of course.
That's why I chose him. I could hardly say

it was a whore and a pimp made me think.

Seattle Blues

It was an envelope of water. It was
a place my life forked, my mind splintered, my soul

went black and blue. But, once or twice, there was Otis
of the long ponytail, of the springy walk

through Pioneer Square. Of the wide-
brimmed hat pulled down low, of the long face

arranged into a mask
of exquisite pain. He sang the blues,

and I can remember, even now, the exact
shape of his penis, how it curved up and away

from surprisingly thin hips. *Don't go,* he'd said, that last
morning, as the tremolo of light

washed in from over the water. *Oh, baby . . . please . . .
don't . . . go . . .*

How little I was sure of then, how easily
I came and went. And yet, I can't help but think

there was some virtue in it. There was, always, his voice,
the sweet shaft of it, sinking way down

to where it hurt, and if, later, he rocked me
way out there, over the water, it was only

because I believed, *I truly believed*
in the fact of his smooth, white skin, in the way

our bodies would curve
over absolutely everything—the speckled city, those horns

that blew—paused—then blew, again, from somewhere beyond
an everlasting fog.

The Way the Body

I

In Catholic school, we were all obsessed
with the body, not the soul. This question

repeated endlessly: *At the Second*
Coming, when we get our bodies back, what

age will we be? It would make each nun, each
year, turn purple in the face, grind her teeth.

At your best age, in the prime of your life.
It seemed fair enough. If you had to grow

old, and creep up the steps as those folks at
Mass did, at least, when you returned, you could

run again, play ball with the best of them.
But I always suspected the nuns lied.

II

I suppose that's why, in my dream of death,
the men are in their twenties, the women

middle-aged. I was walking down a long,
white hall. The door of a room stood ajar.

I opened it very slowly, trying
hard to be quiet, the way I was taught.

The room was filled with music, like nothing
I'd heard before—slow and easy, joyous—

like liquid gold, like honey slipping off
the edge. It came from the horns being played

by men sitting cross-legged on a large,
white bed. And the women, much larger

in body but black, also, stood behind,
swaying as they hummed along with the song.

One turned, smiled at me, and said, *Where you been,*
girl? We done thought you gone. The white flower

pinned to her hair, the voice—it was Billie,
and she was landlady of this place.

Hers was the voice behind the beat, playing
around with it, and hers was the voice

in perfect control of itself, at last.

III

The way the body will follow the mind:
I am being carried on a white stretcher

down the long, narrow hallway of my new
apartment building, while my body goes

into shock from a massive loss of blood.
Hemorrhaging from my womb, I am growing

fainter by the minute, but my mind is
terribly lucid, in spite of it—*This*

is the dream. I must be going to die.
I am pleasantly disintegrating.

But the sound of my son, weeping, pulls me
back to the needful world—I am afraid.

The way the bodies of strangers will fit
into what is missing: the man comforts

my son: *Don't worry. Your mom's gonna be*
okay. Ever been in an ambulance

before? You can sit up front with me.
And you can even turn the siren on.

The way the bodies of strangers come close,
lean over us, whisper, sing—whatever it is

we so desperately need.

Among the Trees

Out here, among the trees, I am often
happy for no reason. Among the blossoms,
yellow on red, a swallowtail, then a hummingbird, its body
a blurred green sheen. The trees
talk to themselves, and I, I merely listen.
I do not suffer the long horizon.

I keep the trees close. Is this
what my father meant, is this the happiness
they fought for? Crusaders, he and the others
who gathered together, each perched on a blood-red
bar stool, reliving the war, the trip to Tokyo after, where the
  children,
he never tired of explaining, ate out of garbage cans.

It was a dark cave we entered each Saturday
after catechism class, a buzzer at the door, rows
of bottles lined up behind the men, facing them, blazing.
It was a place haunted
by a man covered with freckles, a man whose hands
never stopped shaking, whose mouth drooled, a man

my father called Red. *He's shell-shocked. Don't*
be afraid. Just take the chips and soda.
Red, now—you don't understand—he sacrificed.
Red. There was a round red sun
on the flag at home, the one stashed in a box
in the basement, its white silk sky

covered with sailors' signatures, little black squiggles
like birds spun suddenly around
by a great white heat. There were flak jackets, dead
grenades, and there were helmets—all olive green—
there were helmets
shallow enough to fit a child's head.

Letter from Yaddo

So they rolled you into the river, did they, Wayne,
in the cold blue light of the moon? I told you
to quit cruising those bars on Hennepin, I warned you—
But life is so boring, you said. *I must have my gold.*

Bracelet dangling from a trembling wrist. *I must get more*
medication. Unshaven face. *I've been up for*
two or three days now, and the whores
take MasterCard, did you know that? How would I

know that, Wayne? But I know you were my godsend
those long nights in the computer room
we tended to the queen—an IBM mainframe
humming as you spun your tales—lies, no doubt, about

the intricate sex lives of artists, but it whiled away
the boredom of that monstrous room, that belly
of a whale. *Mozart,* you said, *was the worst.*
He was known to . . . But Wayne, where are you

now? In the place with steel bars, the place we all fear.
Is it restful there? Was it like crawling under a tent
of the grownups' overcoats? I am going out now, Wayne,
for a walk, a walk with the trees, and you're welcome

to come. They claim Poe walked these woods, too, shouting—
Nevermore! His death was mysterious, as they all
are. I think we should have flown to Havana, Wayne, on your
gold card. I think we should have smoked those cigars,

those big, fat cigars, smoked them all up, in your leaky boat.

Night Sky, Iowa

What if I just go crazy or something?

He turned from the sky to look at me.

He was grinning, always grinning, when he
was afraid. Then he squeezed my hand. *Good girl.*

Holding hands, we continued to sit there,
breathing in the humid air of August,
of a slowed-down college town.

The trees swayed.

Shoulder to shoulder, on someone's front stoop,
while someone slept. The cicadas were done
going nuts. And those lovely stars, such a

long way off.

I owe you, he said. *I owe you big time.*

It felt good. To love a man. To save his life.

After the Disaster

I let the sheet fall. It's already hot.

The light builds fires in the windows.

Zelda in the nuthouse: I wonder
if she felt betrayed, if she was heartbroken,
if she suffered in the fire.

I can hear the wooden stairs creak
under his weight. He takes two at a time.

Or did she die quietly, breathing in
the smoke, unaware? There's a statue

of Scott in Rice Park, now. Under his weight.

I wish they would just go ahead and fall down.

Under his weight. The fires are rising.

Then no one could get to me ever again.

Magic Houses

I think it must have been the house on Marcy Street,
when snow covered the yard like sleep, when he rose early
to write and, before beginning, would place two fat towels
beneath his typewriter so I wasn't disturbed
in my dreams. And when I did wake, I would lie there
as long as I could, squeezing my bladder muscles,
listening to him whistle as he bounced along,
with that penguin walk of his, to the kitchen
for more coffee. And when, at last, I did get up
to pee, I would sneak up behind him to plant
a kiss on that wild head of dark hair. I keep
wondering how it changed. Was it the house? Maybe
the houses, themselves, own the magic, and that's why
it stays with the house when we leave. I wonder
who lives there now, and are they as happy as we
once were—if the woman, appearing quite nude
at the bedroom door in the morning, brings a look
of delight to the man's eyes, a sense that nothing more
will ever be needed in this world, or beyond.

Three

The Confession

Tell me the truth, he would say. *You're really*
from Venus, aren't you? Who is fooling who?

Would I lie? That emptiness he always
complained about, in the vicinity

of his heart, that's right where we removed it.
Don't want no dead men making trouble, do

we? On Venus, we don't care much for heart.
Oh, we know all about country music,

how, in a song, your heart falls to pieces.
But I have no intention of paying

for any crime. No, siree. On Venus,
we don't even eat. We disassemble

our limbs, we put them on backwards. It helps
to see your planet in a different

light. On Venus, it is so dark, always.
We decorate ourselves with tiny lights.

Colored strings. It makes us feel happy. We need
each other in inexplicable ways.

We do not forget the protoplanet.
And we remember the stars, their many

and bone-chilling deaths—also the era
of nebula, the gas and the sweet dust.

His sin was to envy his own lack of
distinction. But you are like ants to us

on Venus. Talent means nothing at all.
We take the young first, they are so bound by

narcissism. On Venus, it's far too
simple. Anyone can decide, study

the mirror. I picked him, that's all. I can't
tell you just why—he walked like a penguin,

lied too often, convinced himself, because
of the music, that he loved everyone.

I picked him, that's all that matters. He saw
me standing behind the mirror, and he

could not keep his body from trembling in
that awful way. Maybe he was sorry

at the end, maybe not. I will never
know. On my way out, he called me a bitch.

On Venus, we won't speak of it. We give
all there is to give, without a regret.

Here, take my arms of glass—they are for you.
They shatter as you try to handcuff me.

Come morning, you will find nothing you can
recognize: a white gown dropped on the floor,

gas, dust, a solitary string of lights
that won't work when you hold them in your hands.

Stations

I

Crossing another river,
I crawl up the bank, dripping.

Dripping what?

Why, blood, of course.

II

Turning to run
back up the steps, I swivel, then kick
the glass door of your face
with the heel of my boot.

And there you are, in pieces, on the floor.

III

Why am I such a bitch?

You tell me.

You don't know?

Then I'll tell you.

For the power, the long elegant line of it.

IV

Clinging
to the girders
of a railroad drawbridge,
I can't make myself
look down,
but the man, the man is
strong, the man is showing me
just how strong he can be,
the man
is pressing himself
against me, his cock hard, the man
is beginning
a long, drawn-out kiss . . .

Does he enjoy this?

Why, yes. Yes, he does.

V

In black heels
and evening dress, I am trembling
like a winded bird
caught high, helpless
against the scattered lights
of Seattle.

Does he enjoy this?

Why, yes. Yes, he does.

VI

I am terrified of heights,
so I cling to him. And he,

he has a good job with the railroad.

As did his father before him,
as will his son, after.

The long, elegant line of men.

VII

And I am trembling
at the edge of a bridge
that has slowly risen
into the very blackness of the night—
it stands up, erect,
amid the swirling
avenues of fog.

And I am still dangling.

VIII

It rises to let a ship pass.

A phantom ship.

For there is no ship.

There is only power, fear, and fog.

IX

If I let myself drop, I will pass
through the long evening
alone.

Alone, in the fog.

I will fall
sweetly
through the centuries.

X

For I can no longer
recognize myself: fame, fortune, a villa
by the sad sea . . .

And the sun, each afternoon, it shines
so extravagantly

upon the fig tree, swelling
his favorite fruit.

XI

For your troubles, dear, here—
have a fig. No, I did not

doctor them in the night.

XII

Like Jacob of old, my own
sweet son
will absolve me.

Exalt me.

For I am his mother, the root
of all power.

XIII

Because his
was the only love
I was rock-hard sure of.

XIV

Because, for a goddess, there can be no consequence.

The Land of Ugly Pants

In the land of ugly pants
lived a man with no soul that I could ever find,
but around his crotch there spread
a constellation of tiny holes
where pot seeds had landed
after exploding from his overloaded joints
and melting the pea green fabric.
                                        "That's a dead giveaway,"
I said to him once. "Why don't you wear Levis
like everyone else?" "Because," he said,
"they make my balls sweat."
                                        The odd thing is, even
after all those years in Xanadu, I don't
remember his balls, the shape of his cock,
nor the feel of them, for that matter. Our easy,
early nakedness with each other
turns blank as exposed film.
                                        All I can see
is what he threw at the wall, what stuck there:
tiny seeds of tomato mixed with mayo—
a pinkish swirl like a confection, like
early menstruation—a sordid display,
surely.
                                        What I was left with
was less than zero: an empty bankbook,
a cold house, broken teeth, purpled skin, thirteen
stitches to the back of my head, each one
a blackbird's tiny tracking.
                                        Quite simply,
he was not the genius he claimed to be.

Waiting for Venus to Stop It

I am an old woman, her skin turning reptilian
as I sit in the sun, day after day, considering
an empty horizon. I am a mother
of the desert, and I wait for my old buddy, Venus.
It is our day to play cards.

The lion I stole from St. Jerome
lies at my feet, snoring, her jungle days long gone.
At last, the goddess arrives, wearing her store-bought boobs,
heavily made-up, as usual.
What a production!

How she depends upon
the dramatic entrance. *My dear,* I begin the lecture.
Oh, shut up! she says. *You don't know
anything about it.* And, though she is vicious
as ever, I know she is right.

Myself, I depend upon
her obnoxious company, upon the scarves
blowing in a wind that ceased blowing eons ago,
upon the planets circling her skull, and upon the
    hieroglyphics,
yes, those, most of all. I shuffle and deal.

I prefer stud, and call it so, but it seems
each face I turn up on the table is a face she has known,
and known intimately. How tragic for her. How
truly sad. She breaks down and weeps
the big gobs of tears

she is famous for,
and I can't help but take advantage. Yes, I do it.
I slip the ace up my sleeve—diamonds—to save her, I will claim
later. She may never learn, poor girl, but I
sure hope to.

Into the Arms

Into the arms of an old friend, an old
enemy. Not to be easily
confused with an old god,

his other side.

The dancing is all over now, dear John,
dear John. Into the arms of an aqua
sea. Don't think of me,

for I am gone.

Into the arms of that celestial blue.
The prairie sky will blaze before nightfall.
We Yankee girls have no

manners, you said.

So here is the farewell, the glove, the wave.
As my boat pulls away, as you turn back.
A near miss, the oldest

story there is.

Easter

Do the tulips appear on Tulip Street?
Of course, they do. April Fool's and two years
since we fled the Red River Valley, part
of the exodus snaking out of town
as the floodwaters broke through the dikes and rolled
over just about everything, leaving
a thin layer of garbage on the flattest
of lands. Treeless, windy, downright brutal.

Missiles, naked land, gigantic airplanes
looming against the night, spotlighted
in nightmare proportion—*they are so huge*—
as I drove into the air force base, one more
evacuee. The dikes were all failing,
the bridges were out. The guard kept order
and soon the president, himself, would appear
to call us brave, name us heroes of the plains.

Not me. I will hardly forget the *thwunk thwunk*
of helicopter blades filling the night
and that terror of knowing the black water
was rising, overflowing, moving
irrevocably, invisibly, west
and flight was the only course left, and flight
was called for, and yet, and yet—even when
the engineers sat down, put their faces

in their hands and wept, even when the mayor's
voice, coming over the radio, cracked—

even then, it was hard to leave it all
behind. I must have known I would not
go back. Another scattering, and then
the bird with a thing in her beak, a *thing*
because that is what we understand, what
we truly love: the equipage of our world.

Wings

In the final analysis,
everything that exists is a miracle.
—Kafka

They fly from me, they flee. I am running
and running through tall, wet grass, and then

I stop, stoop down, and cup my trembling hands
over the purple alfalfa blossoms.

Their wings beating against the cage of me.

But I wake into a moonlit room
in a noisy city. It was but a dream

made from memory and they are gone,
nearly extinct now. In less than half

a century. Does that make me ancient?

That I can remember the most frail
and sunlit of creatures? That I witnessed,

in my small, cupped palm, a shimmering dust?
That I endure, purposeful, in this summer

of our disbelief, while they do not?

Her Name Was Becky

Her name was Becky, and when she leaned over me, I was saved.
Saved by intervention human, but presently I am saved

by intervention divine: the sun appearing
after days of rain, even snow, in April, and for the first

time in a long time, the smell of sex on my crotch.
I shall not bathe. The smell is like a long-lost love—

a youth of wet secrets, of delirious trembling, of a body
played like a harp. I shall keep it close, let it age

until it reeks. Even if the sperm go dead and useless.
Even so. Even then, I love the smell of *commingling.*

But I meant to tell of Becky in her manly uniform
of brown, bending over me and keeping her voice even and calm

as she took the vital signs, as she snapped quick orders to the men
in their identical brown shirts and pants. As the blood
          kept flowing

from my womb, as they lifted me onto a stretcher and carried
me down the winding hall, it was not their muscle power

but her assurance I clove to
in my fear of dying—cold terror, cold as the discs

taped to my chest—*get the oxygen ready*—
helpless—*a siren blowing through a summer afternoon*—

I watched her face, the face of the woman called Becky, for a clue,
and when it softened in the way a mother's does

when she gazes at her baby, I knew the danger
had passed. The tests showed nothing wrong.

The psychic said it was an abortion of sorts, my body's
attempt to expel the man. *I get a picture of him*

curled up in your womb, comfortable there.
Okay, so I lived, but whenever I begin bleeding again,

for no reason, I wonder if it is another ending, another
beginning. It will be strange to bleed no more.

For twenty years, *the crimson tide, the red equipage,*
has served my psyche well.

In the new country, what will remain?
Wind gods and horsemen, deluge, darkness, mystery—

for it was lust, always lust, which propelled me, and that part
was easy, given the nature of men, given my perpetual

freight, and my streamlined fright, given the moon
and the stars, given those other bodies

all around us, given the whoop and the crying out,
the crash and the thunder, the orbiting, and, of course,

the chance meeting. Given the exquisite, secret light, given
the sizzling heat—most of all, that—the pounding

pulse of it, fire from a windy plateau, a spray of sparks
whirling in the rush of your coming.

But it is quietly, how you go.

Notes

The Cage
Stanza 3: Sappho.
Stanza 6: Billie Holiday.

Golden Gate
Stanza 2, line 2: addresses a poem by Czeslaw Milosz.

With Ferns around Her Face
Stanzas 12–13: Kenneth Clark, "Leonardo da Vinci."

The Spirit of William Speaking to the Spirit of His Wife
Final line: Blake.

The Occasional Mystic
Lines 7–10: Oliver Sacks, *The Man Who Mistook His Wife for a Hat,* especially "The Visions of Hildegard."

Autumn in Ohio, Thinking of James and Another
Stanzas 2–3: James Wright.
Stanzas 5–6: reference to a Mardi Gras story recounted by Elton Glaser.

The Telephonist
Lines 4–5: The Gospel of John.

Poem for the Black Whore in That Bar on PIke Street
Stanza 6: my adaptation of Wallace Stevens, "The Snow Man."

After the Disaster
F. Scott and Zelda Fitzgerald. Scott, a native of St. Paul, Minnesota, has recently been honored by his hometown.

Stations
Sections X–XIV: Robert Graves, *I, Claudius.*

Easter
The Red River flood of April 1997.

About the Author

Susan Yuzna, a native of Minnesota, teaches writing at the University of North Dakota. She has a BA in English from the University of Iowa and an MFA in Creative Writing from the University of Montana. Her first book, *Her Slender Dress,* won the Akron Poetry Prize and the Norma Farber First Book Award from the Poetry Society of America. She has held a Bush Artist Fellowship and the Richard Hugo Memorial Poetry Scholarship, and has been a resident at several artist colonies, including Yaddo and MacDowell.

About the Book

Pale Bird, Spouting Fire was designed and typeset by Kachergis Book Design of Pittsboro, North Carolina. The typeface, Columbus, was designed by Patricia Saunders in 1992 for Monotype Typography.

Pale Bird, Spouting Fire was printed on fifty-five-pound Writers Natural and bound by McNaughton & Gunn, Inc. of Saline, Michigan.